IT'S TIME TO EAT APPLE CABBAGE SLAW

It's Time to Eat
APPLE CABBAGE SLAW

Walter the Educator

Silent King Books
A WhichHead Entertainment Imprint

Copyright © 2024 by Walter the Educator

All rights reserved. No part of this book may be reproduced in any manner whatsoever without written per- mission except in the case of brief quotations embodied in critical articles and reviews.

First Printing, 2024

Disclaimer

This book is a literary work; the story is not about specific persons, locations, situations, and/or circumstances unless mentioned in a historical context. Any resemblance to real persons, locations, situations, and/or circumstances is coincidental. This book is for entertainment and informational purposes only. The author and publisher offer this information without warranties expressed or implied. No matter the grounds, neither the author nor the publisher will be accountable for any losses, injuries, or other damages caused by the reader's use of this book. The use of this book acknowledges an understanding and acceptance of this disclaimer.

It's Time to Eat APPLE CABBAGE SLAW is a collectible early learning book by Walter the Educator suitable for all ages belonging to Walter the Educator's Time to Eat Book Series. Collect more books at WaltertheEducator.com

USE THE EXTRA SPACE TO TAKE NOTES AND DOCUMENT YOUR MEMORIES

APPLE CABBAGE SLAW

It's time to eat, hooray, hooray!

It's Time to Eat

Apple Cabbage Slaw

A special dish is on display.

Fresh and crunchy, sweet and bright,

Apple Cabbage Slaw tonight!

Green and purple cabbage mix,

Chopped up fine with tasty tricks.

Crispy apples, red and sweet,

Make this slaw a healthy treat.

A drizzle of dressing, smooth and light,

A tangy splash, it's just right.

With honey, vinegar, and a dash of fun,

The flavors blend, every one!

Take your fork, give it a try,

A bite so crisp, you'll see why.

The crunch, the tang, the sweetness too,

Apple Cabbage Slaw is good for you!

It's Time to Eat

Apple Cabbage Slaw

Carrots add a splash of orange,

A rainbow bowl we all adore.

The colors pop, so bright and grand,

A tasty meal you'll understand.

It's great for lunch or dinner time,

This slaw will make your tummy light.

It's good for sharing, that's the key,

A dish for friends and family!

Eating healthy is such a treat,

With veggies crisp and apples sweet.

Every bite's a happy song,

It's Time to Eat

Apple Cabbage Slaw

Apple Cabbage Slaw can't go wrong!

When the bowl is empty and clean,

We'll dream of slaw in shades of green.

Tomorrow's lunch, we'll make some more,

Apple Cabbage Slaw to adore!

So grab your fork and don't delay,

It's slaw time now, hip, hip, hooray!

Cabbage and apples, fresh and raw,

It's Time to Eat

Apple Cabbage Slaw

It's time to eat Apple Cabbage Slaw!

ABOUT THE CREATOR

Walter the Educator is one of the pseudonyms for Walter Anderson. Formally educated in Chemistry, Business, and Education, he is an educator, an author, a diverse entrepreneur, and he is the son of a disabled war veteran. "Walter the Educator" shares his time between educating and creating. He holds interests and owns several creative projects that entertain, enlighten, enhance, and educate, hoping to inspire and motivate you. Follow, find new works, and stay up to date with Walter the Educator™

at WaltertheEducator.com

www.ingramcontent.com/pod-product-compliance
Lightning Source LLC
LaVergne TN
LVHW052010060526
838201LV00059B/3950